Camino Poems

Camino Poems

Reflections on the Way
From St. Jean Pied-de-Port to Finisterre

Newton Smith

Manufactured in the United States of America
Argura Press paperback original
FIRST PRINTING

DESIGNER: Katana Lemelin
COVER PHOTO: June Smith
INTERIOR PHOTOS: June Smith and Tony Carroll

Grateful acknowledgement to the editors of the following publications, in which
the poems appeared previously, sometimes in slightly different form: *Asheville
Poetry Review:* "Shadows"; *Pisgah Review:* "Reticence and Silence."

ISBN 978-0-9976614-0-8 (Pbk : alk. paper)

To June
who has always walked with me
the whole
way

Prologue

This book is a collection of poems written as I walked the 500 mile Camino de Santiago Francés in September and early October of 2014. I had always been disappointed in my travel journals before because they never came close to capturing my experience. I decided this time to write poetry instead of my usual narrative descriptions of what I saw, where we stayed, along with a poor summary of historical information. I carried a journal book this time too, but in it I determined to write at least one poem a day. At the top of each poem I recorded where I had been walking when I wrote or started the poem. So in a sense this book is a poetic travelogue.

Walking the Camino was not on my bucket list when our friend, Glenda Bunce, announced that she was going to walk the Way and wanted friends to walk with her. Originally I was not interested even though my wife, June, said she intended to go. I said I'd rather walk from temple to temple in Nepal instead. At some point, however, I found I had decided to go without really knowing why. I caught myself reading books, watching movies and videos, studying maps, making lists of items to carry, and actually training harder than I had been doing on my weekly walks in the Smoky Mountains.

In the midst of preparation I kept asking why I was doing it. It was as if I had been given a call to go rather than deciding logically to do it. I never answered that question until I completed the Camino. Others, I soon realized, also struggled to answer the same question, often all the way to Santiago. In the end the experience of walking the Camino is why we walk it. The Way is a mystery and yet an answer to many of the questions about life I have puzzled over. These poems are a record of my physical, emotional, and aesthetic experience as I walked. They are also a spiritual inquiry into the nature of being human—a physical, thinking being, walking with others on a pilgrimage where each day opens onto new experiences.

I have included maps and other graphics to give a sense of direction and perspective on the route. I have also included a selection of arrows, markers, and photos that provide a bit of the flavor of the walk. The stamps you see on the pages I collected as proof that I had indeed walked the entire way, a requirement in order to get the Compostela certificate in Santiago.

In some ways the first day was literally the high point of the whole pilgrimage. June and I had trained hard, knowing that day would be our biggest challenge. Going over the Pyrenees and entering Roncesvalles was simply exhilarating. From St. Jean-Pied-de-Port in France, where we started, we climbed 4,757 feet and reached the church at Roncesvalles with about 200 beds, walking a total of 17.98 miles adjusted for climb. The views were beyond our expectation and going over the top, drinking from Roland's fountain, and taking the steep decent by mistake, all added up to what I realized at the end was the peak experience of the entire route.

We met Glenda and her friend, Anne Cushman, in Pamplona. We all walked at different paces. June and Glenda often walked together, and Anne would start later, which meant that I was usually ahead of them as we headed to the albergue or hostel where we would sleep. As a result I spent a lot of the time walking alone in silence or at least until I caught up with another pilgrim. When we arrived we usually washed our clothes, ate, wrote in our journals, talked with other pilgrims and went to bed early. Typically, we began before breakfast and walked until we got hungry. We then walked until it was lunchtime. By about 2 or 3 we had reached our destination where we were to sleep. A typical day averaged about 12 miles and might go through two or more villages or towns as well as well-traveled woodland trails. The walking was not excessively strenuous once our bodies got accustomed to the daily routine. Of course there were blisters, knee issues, and possible shin splints, and other ordinary pains. June, however, suffered a stress fracture in her ankle near the peak at Cruz Ferro but still walked the last 80 miles to Santiago in considerable pain not knowing that it was a fracture until we got home.

Because it was September we experienced nature's gifts of ripening fruit. Many days I gleaned blackberries, grapes, apples, figs, peaches and other fruit and chestnuts along the way. The countryside was in full harvest, and vineyards and wheat fields lined our path much of the way. It meant that my attention was focused on the abundance of this earth instead of on my narrow self and its minor concerns. My attention often fell on butterflies, snails, anthills and the abundance of rocks. Part of the Camino traverses the Meseta, the high plains area dominated by vast fields of wheat. Here emptiness and silence became an opening, a recognition that we are held in a space that extends beyond all we can imagine.

Many days I walked with new friends, bonding in ways that take years back at home. Sometimes our conversations spanned English, Spanish, French or German, and one day I listened to a blind woman describe what she perceived to her companion who was leading her with a sash. Because we were all experiencing the body's aches, compassion and willingness to help was the norm. Encouragements were everywhere, from the greeting, "Buen Camino," to the notes tacked to trees urging the tired walker to continue. Once, I encountered a series of rose petals leading up a particularly steep hill. Locals were very eager to point out the way in towns where the directions were confusing. And the signs and arrows put up by those who traveled the Way before us marked every turn or intersection, so it was easy to find where we were to go.

Many of these poems are addressed to you, the reader. Some poems involve me talking to myself. One is in the voice of a medieval pilgrim who has blazed the way for contemporary walkers. Most are simple reflections. At the end is a song I wrote and sang to myself as I walked to keep the pace. All of these poems are meant as an offering to those who have walked or want to walk the Camino. Thank you for being my companion on this pilgrimage.

Table of Contents

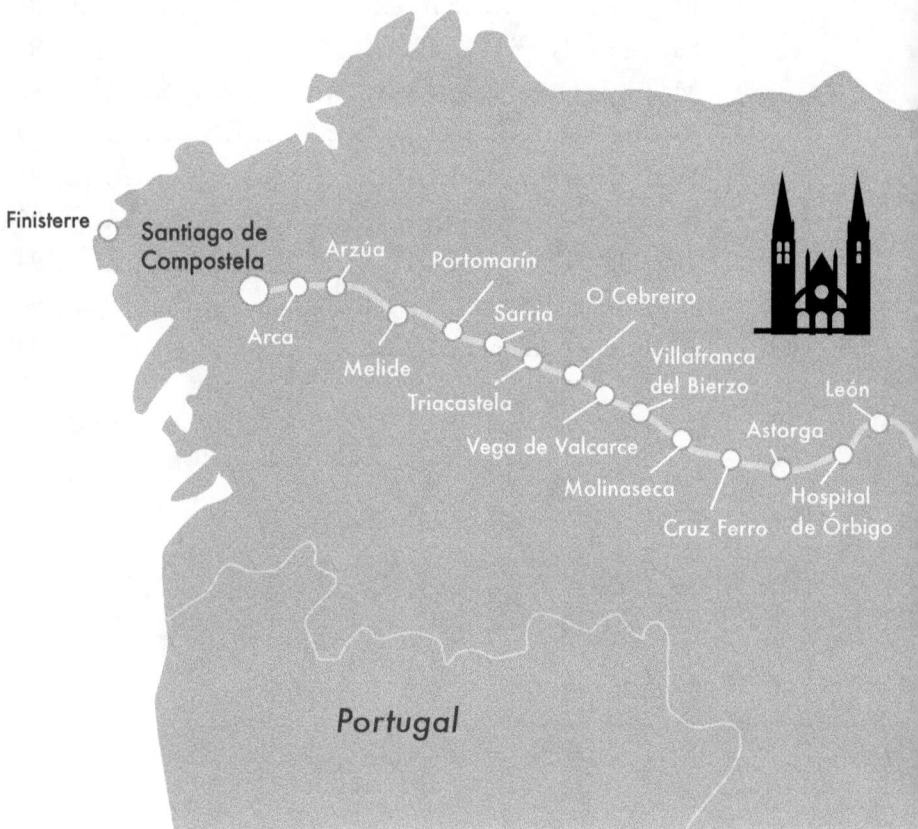

Finisterre

Santiago de
Compostela

Arzúa

Portomarín

Arca

Sarria

O Cebreiro

Melide

Villafranca
del Bierzo

Triacastela

León

Vega de Valcarce

Astorga

Molinaseca

Hospital
de Órbigo

Cruz Ferro

Portugal

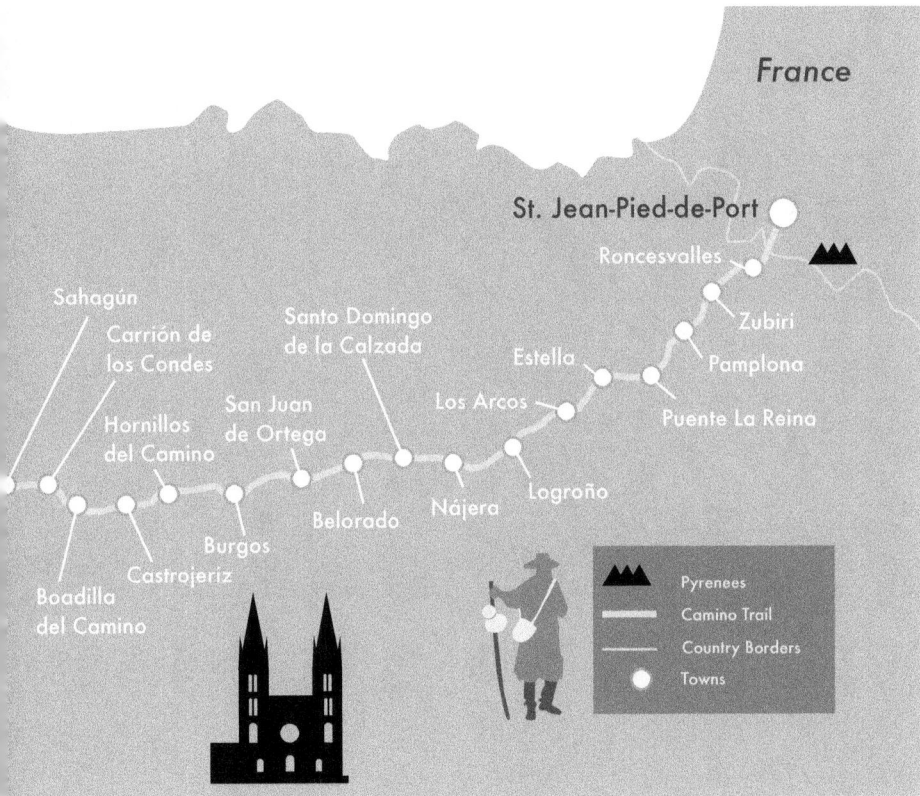

France

St. Jean-Pied-de-Port

Roncesvalles

Sahagún

Santo Domingo
de la Calzada

Zubiri

Carrión de
los Condes

Pamplona

Estella

San Juan
de Ortega

Los Arcos

Puente La Reina

Hornillos
del Camino

Belorado

Nájera

Logroño

Burgos

Castrojeriz

Boadilla
del Camino

Pyrenees
Camino Trail
Country Borders
Towns

Deciding to Go

Here you are holding this book about the Camino,
not sure how you came to this point.
In front of you are lists,
a pile of hiking gear catalogues,
and notes about how to prepare.
"Five hundred miles?" you ask yourself.
"What led to this? When did you decide?"
You begin a mental pilgrimage
tracing the steps to what you assume was
a rational sequence of thought.
Soon you have entered a space
where logic and words don't apply,
a catacomb where the bones
of your past are buried, the crypt
where the treasures you have
clutched are hidden from view.
Here are your parents and grandparents,
your teachers, all those who warned
you or encouraged you,
also your dreams and nightmares,
and all those fading moments
you swore you'd never forget.
Here too are sinews and urges
and the long memory of the body.
This is the cabal that decided
what you will do next
before you knew it.
Here you see your finger
like a saint's relic pointing
not at heaven or even at you
but beyond to a place
where you will go
without knowing why,
your Camino.

Before Departure

What is this walking all about?
We knew how to walk before
so why now will we go so far
and for so many days to reach
a distant cathedral in a remote
part of the world?

In preparation we leave
behind clothing and gear
that we normally would take
so that we can walk lightly
and shed the burden
of our possessions.

All this training
we hope will take us over
the hard climb into
a new place where
what we seek
is what is here, now.

What we seek
is already ours
if only we take time
to be right now
instead of when or then
and here instead of there.

You Know the Way

St. Jean Pied-de-Port

Before it was always later.
You heard about the way
but said not now for years.
What names did they call it?
The Tao, the Dharma,
the Hadj, the Camino?
There were a lot of them.
They were all hard,
long and unsettling,
like nothing you'd
ever done before.
But now, as if by
a temple bell
or cathedral bell
you were called.
So you made plans:
maps, books, purchases
and reservations.
Useless. You can't prepare.
Though it is an ancient path
others have walked before,
for you everything will be new.
You will climb mountains,
walk through pastures and fields,
and pass shrines and churches.
What you see on the way
is not what matters.
Forget remembering.
The way is walked
from the inside
in deep silence.
It will scorch your soul.
You will lose your way
and return again and again.
Where you're going
others have traveled,

but none the way you'll go.
Here you are now.
This first step
will change your life.
Now begin.

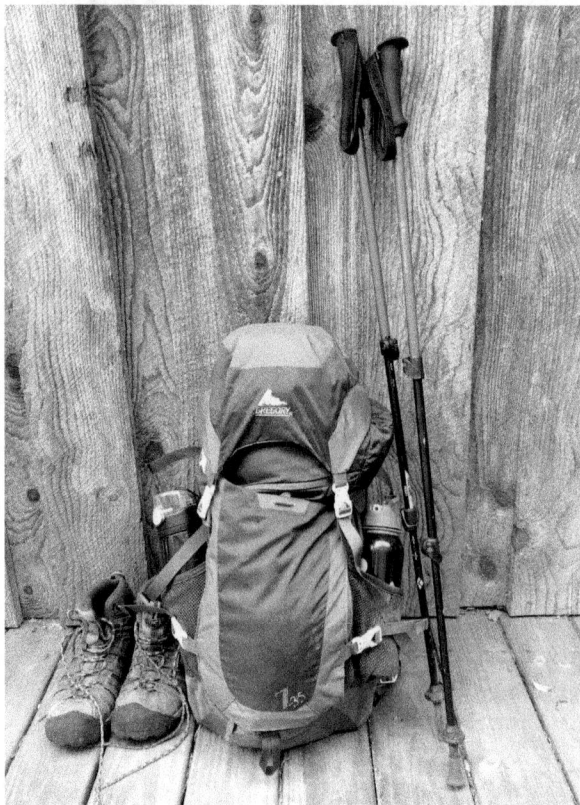

From St. Jean Pied-de-Port to Pamploma

Words Float Away

St. Jean Pied-de-Port to Col de Lepoeder

A new sun wakes up the world,
uncovering what has not been seen before.
The green rises up as mountains,
its color like sea waves in the morning light.
The sheep on the hills no longer puffy dots
but radiant and glowing with white.

To walk here is to take a sacred path
whose stones were turned to gravel by ancient feet.
The very ground sparkles with an inner light.
The cows, silhouetted against the grass,
occur outside of thought, as if
they were new creations just birthed.

The winds pluck the leaves
and lift them and all our thoughts
into the air like the ten thousand things
suddenly apparent swirling all around.
Words float away and ideas disappear.
All that remains is a wordless silence.

The fog that rose up the mountain now clears,
exposing the layered peaks beyond this horizon
revealing a different life unfolding like a map.
From here we walk in mystery
where each step opens into a new dimension
and we enter our life for the first time.

Through the Gate
St. Jean Pied-de-Port to Roncesvalles via Route de Napoleon

Past the gate, those who climb
meet their naïve intentions
like the wind blowing in their face.

High above are the jumbled peaks
that will strain all endurance.
Unfamiliar pains will stir up dread.

The mountains are dotted with ten thousand sheep
so far away they look like white flowers
scattered among the green pastures.

The azure sky holds the burnished sun
like a golden nugget on a velvet cloth
and the landscape becomes a postcard.

Climbing deeper and deeper
along the crooked path up,
presuppositions drop like fall leaves

and all hope of rescue disappears.
Courage is all that remains, feeble as it is,
and the breath that barely keeps coming.

Where this path leads is a mystery.
It is a call to a new way of living
where half lives become whole.

The climb calls for attentive silence.
Gradually the distant sheep and cows
and farmsteads awaken in a fresh, new world.

Fog drifts down from the peaks
and out of the white mist
a white horse emerges as a sign.

Near the crest is a fountain of water,
cold on the teeth and sweet to the tongue,
a blessing for those who seek a higher path.

At the top there is no way left
but down. Accept all that is
most difficult in your life,

surrender to the recognition
that your pain is just a small part
of the whole world's suffering.

Here you will find your bed among
strangers and would-be saints,
a communion of pilgrims on the Way.

Each will begin the next day in the dark
without a rehearsed story or expectations,
prepared to face whatever the path unveils.

In the Dark
Roncesvalles to Espinal

We always begin in darkness
no matter how many torches we hold.
The maps we carry as guides
do not assure us as we walk
and are pointless without light.
We look for signs, arrows to point the way,
but stumble over stones and roots.
We think we know the way,
but what we think won't guide our feet.
All that matters now is right here.
Each step leads beyond where we are,
beyond what we know, somewhere else.
Stop. This is where we are now.
Beyond is in the dark.
The blazes we look for
were made in the dark
for those who walk this dark way
by those who walked in darkness before.

The Abundance of Stones

Espinal to Zubiri

The way is strewn with stones—
gravel, river rock, shale, and paving stones.
At first no one looks up for fear of falling.
Each step is considered, hesitant
and taken in the hope of safety.
Looking up is hard.
Yet the verges of the path are heavy
with fruit: blackberry, elderberry,
and wild plums, rose hips,
hawthorn fruit and even holly berries
rise out of these stones at our feet.
The fruit of these stones
feeds us as we glean along the way.

The Bridge
Zubiri to Pamplona

We walked today on a Roman road
crossing an ancient bridge
into a suburb of Pamplona where once
a fulling mill straddled the river.
The road was cobbled with stones
that would shatter the teeth of those
who rode in chariots from Rome.
The delicate arches of the Romanesque bridge
were formed by ancient engineers.
The soldiers who gathered stones,
the masons who built the arches,
the men who formed the dam and sluices,
and the farmers who brought the wool
have all vanished outside of history.
Today this town is celebrating
and demonstrating for Basque independence,
an ancient cause again going nowhere.
We follow the river past this place,
look back at the arches of the bridge
and know that all this too will drift down stream
along with us who walk this way.

From Pamplona to Burgos

Stones and Words

Pamplona to Puente la Reina

Some men leave stones—
bridges, roads, structures,
in hopes their names
will live as monuments.
The stones last, their names
disappear with time.
Others leave words,
mere scribbles on pages white.
Today we cross bridges
built by nameless Romans,
but talk of Lorca,
Jimenez, Rumi and Hafiz.

A Meditation on the Body
Puente la Reina to Estella

A pilgrimage starts in the body.
At first the steps are easy,
nearly an ordinary walk,
but then the breath
becomes your focus
as you pant your way
up hill.

Soon breathing in
and breathing out
takes all your attention.

Later the stones along the way
turn your thoughts to feet.
Your mind quits thinking
and becomes a contemplation
on stones and roots.

Body part by body part
announce themselves.
Places you've long ignored
or never known
scream for attention.
Every night you tend
to blisters with a surgeon's skill.

Whatever you thought before
about why you took this way
is now obscured by the body's concerns.

What you know now
is that this body
will break down.

The hills and stones
are now a part of your bones.

You are a pilgrim.
Welcome each day as a guest.
Then walk on, walk on.

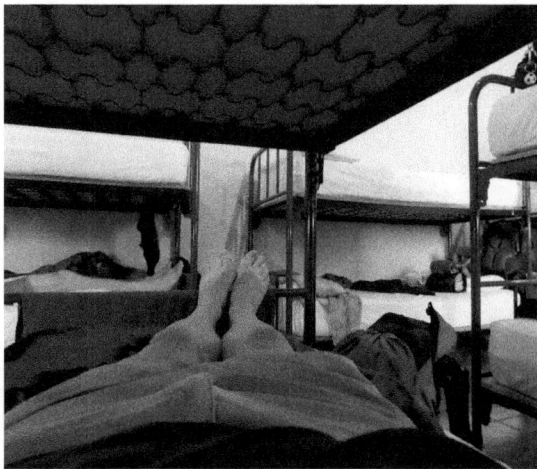

Walking Alone
Estella to Villamayor de Monjardin

You stayed behind as I walked
to Irache where a fountain pours wine
not water for Pilgrims on the Way.
There no one truly walks alone.

I raised a toast to your
health and happiness
and tried not to think
how today you are not here.

Later the walkers
spread out so that each
found their own pace
and most walked alone.

With no one in sight
I turned to look back for you
knowing you were coming,
but you weren't there.

Later after offering each
step and each breath to you
who would meet me soon,
I realized I had not walked alone.

Moonlight

Villamayor de Monjardin to Los Arcos

In the moonlight
edges disappear
and objects fade
into the silver glow.
No shadows ahead
or behind to remind
me of myself.
Instead I walk
in a blue pool
of light under
a shimmering sky.
When the sun comes,
so does my shadow.
It follows me
or is all I see ahead.
The moon is still
in the sky.
Let me walk
in moonlight all day.

Wind in My Face

Los Arcos to Logroño

Welcome West Wind.
Come blow in my face.
I know where you come from—
the end of the earth
past where the sun sets.
Soon we will smell the sea
on your breath.
It is where we are headed,
our first and last home.
We've scorched the earth.
Come, cool us
with your breeze.
We know who you are
and still we welcome you.
What else can we do?

Snail's Pace

Logroño to Navarette

On the way to Torres del Rio
small snails were swarming
over the wild anise lining the path.
On their backs each wore a spiral shell.
Today, like snails we have slowed our pace.
Hundreds of Peregrinos have climbed slowly
into this town wearing packs on their backs.
We are learning the lesson snails teach:
the way to Santiago is supposed to be slow.
Each step must be relished,
whether pain-filled or delightful.
Arriving will mean you have consumed
slowly each morsel of the way.
Buen Camino.

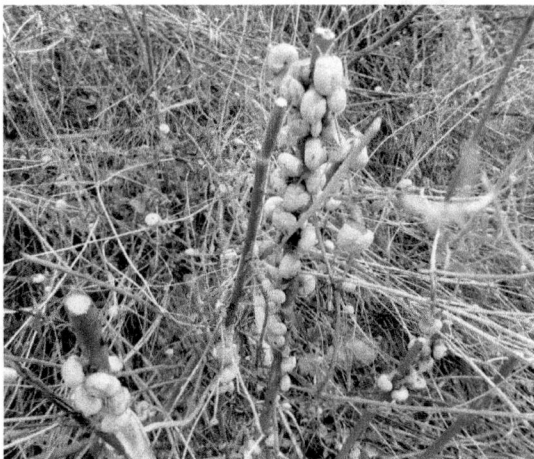

Leaving the Marketplace
Navarette to Azofra

Leaving home and the marketplace isn't easy.
Others who have done it before
left signs to mark the way.
But in towns the directions
lead past bars, places to eat
or shop, and to tables where people
are talking, expecting you.
Worries are around every corner
waiting for you to come,
cower, or do something on a list.
Turn your head, and you'll
lose the way again.
In the countryside, among wheat fields
and vineyards, the way is clear—
a dirt path, leading up this hill
and the one beyond that
all the way to the end.

Stories

Azofra to Santo Domingo de la Calzada

In the legend, a young man
on pilgrimage spurned a woman.
She then hid silver in his pack,
and he was framed and hung.
His parents went on to Santiago, grieving.
They returned to find him alive
still hanging but held up by Saint Domingo.
The magistrate doubted their story
until the chicken he was eating
got up, crowed and flew off the plate.

Do you believe that story?
No? Here is another one.

You get to Santiago and you are forgiven
and your life is changed forever.

Or maybe your story is that you
are responsible for your own salvation?

What story are you telling yourself?
Will it take you all the way to the end?

Bowing to the Sun

Santo Domingo de la Calzada to Belorado

The day began with smells.
The slightly sour scent of wheat stubble,
the deep aroma of turned earth,
and then the allure of blackberries.
How special to have these berries
for breakfast free for the picking
and elderberries too.
Soon I want to taste everything:
rosehips, flowers, thistle,
even the pebbles at my feet.

The breeze lifts my head.
The endlessly changing clouds
seize my attention for a while
and the path becomes only the sound
of my feet walking, crunching the stones.
Then, around a bend, a field
of sunflowers, their heads bent,
as in prayer before the rising sun.
I must bow my head too
and kneel in thanks for this day.

Self-Portrait

Belorado to Villafranca Montes de Oca

I stopped to take a self-portrait
standing on this beautiful hill.
When I turned the lens around
there was no me—
just the wheat fields,
and on the horizon,
a faint rainbow.
How free. How free.

Rose Petals

Villafranca Montes de Oca to San Juan de Ortega

Someone sprinkled rose petals
along my path today.
At first where the trail was steepest
the petals were spaced closer.
As the way became easier,
the petals were dropped further apart.
At one point, when the walk was level,
there were several petals
near a small puddle and then no more.
The petals were like ancient verses
or shrines along the way,
reminders that loving kindness
is the true nature of this path.
No one else saw them,
but they were there.
Look for signs on your way.
Someone will leave them for you, too.

The Path

San Juan de Ortega to Atapuerca

Some mornings the path climbs
so steep you almost give up.
Other days, the trail cascades
down hill convincing you
that you have lost the way.
The hardest is when all is flat,
unchanging fields of wheat
without end, unmarked
and undistinguished.
Here is where it is easy
to lose your way.
Head to where the sun sets.
Your way is into the dark.

Remember

Atapuerca to Burgos

On the hill overlooking Burgos
is a tall wooden cross.
A short distance beyond
is a labyrinth of gathered stones.
Stop here for a while.
Remember that love for all
is the heart of the way,
and that we all spiral
into the center of everything.

From Burgos to Leon

The Inner Path

Burgos to Tardajos

The physical way is blazed in the flesh.
You know where you are
and how far you have gone
by bodily evidence.
Blisters form and heal,
knees ache with each step,
shoulders, hips, and backs
mark each day's progress.
But on the inner path
the signs are less clear.
For moments you have great peace
and lose yourself in all,
floating away with the clouds.
Or you meet someone
who needs to tell you
a new version of their life
so you listen and smile.
Or you lament the life
you have let slip away
as the clouds darken.
Where are the markers
for the inner path?

PENSION
PEÑA
LA PUEBLA, 18-2°
BURGOS | ESPAÑA
19-09-2014

Robin, Sing me a Song

Tardajos to Hornillos del Camino

At La Fuente Praetorre
in the shady grove of trees
you sat strumming
and singing your song
where I came to find water.
I pumped the old fashioned handle,
drank the cool water,
ate my cheese and bread,
and listened to you there.
The other women smiled
and told me their names,
but it was yours I listened for.
I will always remember
how you sang on and on
and imagine you sang for me.

Way Markers

Hornillos del Camino to Hontanas

In cities and the countryside
we look for the yellow arrows
and shells to point the way.
What leads me on
are the elderberry verges,
blackberries leaning over,
the brilliant rosehips,
and hawthorn fruit.
I look for the little yellow flower,
bright as the sun,
and the violet puff balls.
These and the sudden
brilliance of this blue aster
keep me on the way.

Blue Butterfly

Hontanas to San Antón

The path had narrowed
to a single file.
Gone were the berries
that bounded our walk.
Even grass
had become sedge.
Suddenly a startling blue
butterfly flitted
across our path,
as blue as the blue
asters the day before.
Oh, to be led
on the way
by a butterfly,
bluer than the sky.

Shadows
San Antón to Castrojeriz

In the mornings
with the sun behind me
my shadow is tall.
Its long legs
stretch as far
as my ambition.
As the sun climbs
my shadow's legs
grow shorter.
By noon it seems
I am walking in place.
In the afternoon
I have to drag
my shadow behind.
At dark my shadow
has quit, refusing
to move anymore.

White Giants

Castrojeriz to San Nicholás

On every ridge
white giants wave
their long arms
stirring the wind
and warding off invaders.
In the villages
below, the people
are safe.
They turn on their lights
and give thanks.

Witnesses
San Nicholás to Boadillo del Camino

I sit here under grape vines
drooping with ripening clusters,
eating lentil soup, happy
that my wife has arrived.
Pilgrims of all sorts drift in
carrying packs and staffs,
some limping a bit,
others smiling to see friends
recently met have arrived.
How easy it is to form friends
on the Camino where each
is dealing with pain and fatigue
and yet walking on.
Compassion comes natural
here on the Way where our bodies
remind us of impermanence
and the vistas remind us
that we walk as witnesses
to this abundant life.

Dance

Boadilla del Camino to Villarmentero

The plowed fields seem to thrum
as the poplars rustle
like brushes on snare drums.
The willows on the riverbank shimmy
and the sunflowers nod in the wind.
A field of lespedeza
sways to the rhythm,
its purple flowers like sequins
shimmer in the morning light.
What else can one do
but dance?
Hold the world close
and dance, dance, dance.

On the Meseta

Villarmentero to Carrión de los Condes

No two fields are the same.
This one is fresh plowed
and yellow. That one—
last year's wheat stubble
just harrowed in and brown.
Another has lain fallow
for several years.
Each, if you look closely,
is different, like waves
breaking at the horizon.
Close up on the path
ant hills rise up
like dwarf volcanoes.
Tufts of grass tower
over green moss like trees.
Thistles are becoming
ghost gargoyles.
Look away and look back
and all will be different.

Pay Attention

Carrión de los Condes to Calzadilla de la Cueza

Pebbles—grey, brown, striped,
some round, others chat.
Feet crunching, scraping.
Breathing in sync or out.
The breeze rustling
through the willows.
The small purple asters
and a yellow buttercup
startle the eye.
Beyond this path
the hills, furrowed
so the eye stretches out
past horizons.
Thoughts arrive
then float away
with the clouds.
Back to the stones
at your feet.
This is why
you are here.
Pay attention.

This is Enough

Calzadilla de la Cueza to Ledigos

Close your eyes and let the sun
bathe you in light and warmth.
You have walked far enough today.
You have a place to sleep
and there is food nearby.
Feel the breeze wash over
your skin and ruffle your shirt.
Let it all happen as it will
and be aware of it as it happens.
This is enough for now.

Emptiness
Ledigos to Terradillos de los Templarios

Here on the Meseta
the land stretches
in every direction
beyond the horizon.
Objects are swallowed up
in this vista.
What is most apparent
is space
and how it persists.
All objects within it,
including us,
come and then go.
This flower,
this stone,
this hand that writes,
all are held
in this emptiness.

Half Way

Terradillos de los Templares to Sahagún

The monument at Sahagún
said this was the half way point
of the Camino.
I puzzled over what it means.
If the Way is a lifetime
but is also here, now,
where am I in this long
pilgrimage I call my life?

24/09/2014

Where Are You Going?

Sahagún to Calzada del Coto

At dawn streams of pilgrims
flow into the gravel paths,
each with a pack on their back,
setting out on a five or six hour walk
toward a town they can't pronounce
and will remember only from their journal.
Who are these people?
From Australia, Korea, New Zealand,
Iceland, Sweden, England,
Germany, France and Spain,
they seem ordinary—
pharmacists, counselors, teachers,
nurses, property managers, bankers
the recently divorced
and the recently grieved —
the sort you'd meet
in the local grocery store.
But here they are
walking this ancient way.
And who am I
who writes these words—
where am I going?
Why do I so often choose
the more remote options?
And you, who reads these words,
where are you now?
Where are you going?

I Walk Alone

Calzada del Coto to Calzadilla de los Hermanillos

Today I chose the path
away from towns and roads.
It meant I walked alone.
No one in sight,
ahead or behind.
The trail went on and on.
I yearned for company
but none was there.
Just birds, a few oaks for shade,
and gravel at my feet.
Nothing more is needed,
just my attention.
I do this for all of us.

25 / 9/ 14

Earth Orchid

Calzadilla de los Hermanillos to Mansilla de las Mulas

Little flower, I do not know your name.
How strange and beautiful you are.
Your blossoms sit on the ground
with no stem and no leaves around.
It looks as though your flowers
were dropped along the path
from some exotic flower stem.
Your six amethyst petals
open to a white center.
Your blossom is delicate
and tender like an orchid.
When I try to take a blossom,
it is just flower and root.
You have lined my path
all day as if I walked
a prince's way.
I name you Earth Orchid
and take your blessing
home with me.

A Candle Burns for You

Mansilla de las Mulas to Leon

The priest said,
"You know what you have done.
Now make amends on Pilgrimage
to Santiago de Compostela."
He gave me a map, a gourd,
a staff, and a mochila
to carry what I did not wear.
I was afraid those first days,
sometimes hungry,
with no place to sleep
and a body sore all over.
In strange towns men
would point the way,
women would give me bread,
and I slept in churches
and barns and homes
of those who cared for pilgrims.
There were others
on the way too.
Once I counted
hundreds before me
and was told
thousands upon thousands
would follow.
I began helping those who limped,
encouraging those in despair,
showing the way
for those lost,
or needing water,
or a place to stay.
All along the way
I have left markers
for those who come after.
In each church

I have lit a special candle
just for you.
You know what you have done.
A candle burns for you
here on the Camino.

Cathedral Light

Burgos and Leon

At Burgos the sun each day
is revealed through the lacework
of stone and shadow.
The heavy mass reaches up
and traces a filigree in air
as delicate as a spider's web
contains the sun and breeze.
We stand and wonder
who first saw the vision
of this place and how
that bright image
became the light we see now,
emerging through centuries
of craftsmen carving
solid, unyielding rocks
into this final homage to the sun.
At Leon the light is found
in the darkness inside
the nave and transepts.
Looking up, we are drenched
in color. The stained glass
turns familiar stories
into hues of light
we never saw before.
The builders surely beheld
a mystery beyond
what they knew.
We come to these places
yearning for radiance in our lives.
We light candles and votives
hoping that these small embers
will change us and somehow last
centuries as these cathedrals have.

From Leon to Sarria

Don't Stop

Leon to Villar de Mazarife

I have drawn arrows in the sand,
and lined up pebbles
to point the way.
The shells I left to assure you.
It is easy to lose your way,
especially when nothing
seems to change.
I know it is hard.
You begin to wonder
why you have chosen
this difficult path.
Press on and remember,
it does not matter
how slowly you go
so long as you do not stop.
Wherever you go,
go with all your heart.
I will wait for you.
Don't stop.

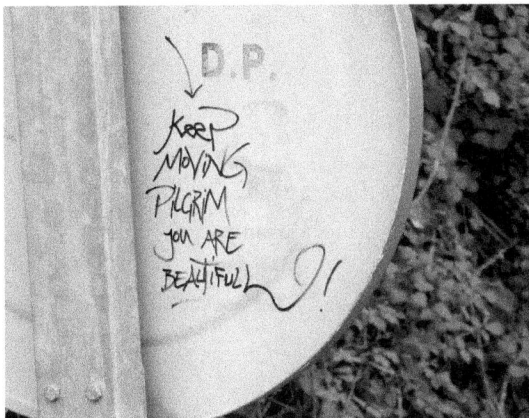

Fig Tree
Villar de Mazarife to Hospital de Órbigo

Your branches invite a climb,
and your leaves are dark enough to hide a boy.
All along the way I have scanned
your limbs to see if your fruit is ripe.
Today, as I wandered the garden
picking up filberts and eyeing apples,
I found myself in the shade of a fig tree.
A young woman stood on a ladder
picking ripe figs and handing them
down to her friend for their basket.
She handed me one to eat.
Oh, your fruit is so sweet.
Your heart is purple and green
and I thank you.

Walk with Me

Hospital de Órbigo to Santibañez de Valdeiglesias

Today we walked together
as the sun rose behind us.
Our paces matched
and the sound of our steps
and poles became a rhythm
accompanying the lilt of your voice
and my bass notes.
We each point out
what attracts us
in the world around us.
Our vistas expand
and our focus becomes acute.
Each moment deepens
and lasts longer than mere time,
and we arrive quicker
than our thoughts.
Walk with me more
on this sacred way.

Prostrations

Santibañez de Valdeiglesias to Astorga

On a hill overlooking Astorga
everything seems close enough to touch.
The cathedral and the Gaudi Bishop's Palace
appear only steps away.

Oh, how easy it is to lose perspective
on the Way, especially when you've walked far.
To actually enter the city is like
a series of prostrations—first down

a steep hill, then up a ramp
resembling a steel scaffold,
and then back to climbing sharply
almost on our knees

until we reach the marketplace
where prostitutes once were
imprisoned near the nunnery
now a hostel for pilgrims.

We visit the dusty, ill-used cathedral
and stroll through the garden at the palace.
Clearly, this is not our destination.
The Way demands more bowing and rising before the end.

Un...
Astorga to El Ganso

How quickly the desirable turns un. . . .
And the pleasant becomes un. . . .
Satisfactory soon is un... too
almost as soon as we say it.
What we desire is never good
enough for long, but maybe, maybe . . . .
And so it goes day after day
wanting the next thing, place, time,
love, sensation we imagine will finally suffice.
Meanwhile each moment passes
unobserved, unnoticed, unfelt
and unlived because we were looking elsewhere.
Should we just undo desire?

No When, No Where

El Ganso to Rabanal del Camino

Ask "when" and the village you saw
moves to the next hill or out of sight.
You will never find the Way
by looking at your watch.

Ask "where" and the Way disappears
around the next corner or mountain.
Asking where turns every place
including the Way to ink spots on a map.

The Way is outside of time.
It is this step you are taking now.
It is the sound of a cricket mid-day.
It is breathing while the heather blooms.

The Way is nowhere to be found.
To look for it is to lose it.
It is this sun on your face.
It is here where the rocks meet your feet.

Ampersand

Rabanal del Camino to Cruz Ferro

At the Iron Cross on the Camino,
I left a typesetter's mark for 'and.'
I had taken it from home because
there is always something more.
You think you are where you meant to be
but you forgot the 'and then.'
You think you understand
and everything is settled…
and then what happens next
undermines all meaning.
It's a good day…and then….
Things are going badly, and then….
My ampersand marks the edge
of what I really know.
Beyond is unknown—
Terra Incognito—
where we usually are
without knowing it.
And then….

&

Help Along the Way

Cruz Ferro to El Acebo

On the Camino everyone has pain.
As a result compassion comes easy.
Today we needed help and other pilgrims came.
One had a phone but no number.
Another had the number but no Spanish.
Then someone showed up who understood us
and could make the call.
A community of internationals
came to our aid.
It is the Camino way.

Words on the Way

El Acebo to Molinaseca

The path was a precipitous stumble
down shale and scree and pebbles.
Just when I had lost hope
I saw a word written on a rock:
"Breathe." A few breaths later
I realized the landscape had changed.
I walked now in a Zen landscape.
Later I read in rocks on the ground:
"Namaste." The gravel underfoot then
whispered, wishing me well.
On one stone someone had written:
"God walks with you."
Then toward the end of the day
I walked with a woman named Novena.
The Way is full of encouragement.
Just listen to what it says.

Pain
Molinaseca to Ponferrada

We think pain takes place in our bodies.
What a narrow setting we choose.
So often the landscape surrounding us
is expansive and intriguing
if we could only observe it.
Here at our feet the grasshopper
is delighting in his ability
to leap so high, so close
to his last few days of fall.
And this flower in the path—
how could anything
be more radiant right here
where this pain occurs?

Thoughts on the Way

Ponferrada to Cacabelos

In the countryside, thoughts are slow,
mostly without words, just noticing
how gardens are different here,
how grape vines are gnarled sometimes
and in rows elsewhere,
how the stones are sometimes
like river pebbles and then
more like shards.

Then no thoughts but listening:
the sound of walking,
the click of the pole,
the whisper of breath.
You smile and breathe deeper
noting that thoughts have left
their storyline and turned
to naming, lists, random phrases.

Figs ripe now.
Strange apples.
Cauliflower?
Call home.
Thirsty.
Shins hurt.
Shin splints?

Then the crunch of feet on gravel.
Thoughts are fleeing
like the scudding clouds.
Not one seems to stay in place.
Back on the Way,
following the arrow.
Thinking: walking, walking, walking.

Who Are We?

Cacabelos to Villafranca del Bierzo

We think we know who we are,
but the Camino tells us we don't.
In the mornings as we start
our bodies are who we are:
its aches, the places that move ok,
the comfortable fit of the pack,
the way our feet meet the path.
Then the mind interrupts,
"Take the steeper route.
The books say it is best."
For a while the mind is in charge
until the trail becomes steep,
and breath is hard, and legs cramp.
Whoever we thought we were
vacillates—mind/body/mind/body.
Meanwhile the way takes us high
above the road, overlooking
mountains on every side
and through a grove of chestnuts.
Then who we are is lost among
all that is here in this place
where what we think and feel
falls like the ripe chestnuts
to the ground where we walk.

Lunch Under Chestnut Trees

Villafranca del Bierzo to Trabadelo

We talk, this new friend and I,
about our children and how every child
needs the experience of the wild
to learn that we humans belong
in the midst of it all—the moon
phases, the mountain ranges,
the autumn's abundance,
and sticks and nuts among the leaves.
We sit enjoying our water,
some fruit, and bread
under a chestnut tree.
In this grove of chestnuts,
farmers are clearing away leaves
in order to harvest the nuts.
This is what we want for all
children and their children too—
to sit against a tree trunk, talk,
eat, and remember those we love.

Friends

Trabadelo to La Portela de Valcarce

Where are they now,
those friends whose faces
lit up your days
like the sun's first rays
when you began together
before dawn early on?
Some have gone on ahead.
Others you've left behind.
You say you'll never forget them,
a vow you've broken time
after time in your lifetime.
Their names are already as faint
as the name of that quaint
town where you ate eggs so rich
they were orange as the setting sun.
Up the next hill is a new friend
waiting to meet you.
Keep walking.
When the sun rises tomorrow,
you'll be fast friends forever.

Camino Churches

La Portela de Valcarce to Vega de Valcarce

We walk from town to town
following arrows, signs, and maps.
Early pilgrims looked for churches,
their bell towers silhouetted
on the horizon at the next hill.
They were landmarks,
a refuge, a reminder
of why they walked.
Here was a place for them,
and a welcome, perhaps food.
Today we walk past,
noting their age and style.
Occasionally, we go in to pray.

Where Water Flows
Vega de Valcarce to O Cebreiro

In Galicia water flows from
every crevice down hill
into small streams
past villages with fountains
for pilgrims on their way.
We stop, fill our bottles,
and climb on to the next town.
On the ridges
we trace the path
the water takes—
down notches, hollows,
valleys, into streams.
Where water flows
trees and grass grow green.
Our lives follow
where water flows.

Reticence and Silence

O Cebreiro to Alto do Polo

Come sit down.
I'll pour you a cup of wine.
It will warm up this room
when outside all is wind and mist.
Drink up and tell me
what brings you here
and where you come from.
No, you speak first.
I am practicing the old Saint's
rule of Reticence and Silence.
You have come a long way,
and I have not heard your story.
Tonight I will dwell in the silences
between your words.

Mist
Alto do Polo to Triacastela

The mist this morning
veils the hills.
Everything is softer, cooler,
mysterious as if something
is not completely revealed.
It is like a romantic painting—
cows grazing, the landscape
a green patchwork quilt.
You are in a distant village,
and thinking of you now
clouds my eyes
as the rain and wind
buffet me on this path alone.
Soon I will catch up
and hold you in my arms
and feel your warmth
as I tell you about
love and wind and mist.

Contemplation

Triacastela to Samos

On the Camino
old injuries come back
for your reflection.
So do the harms, slights
and indifference
you inflicted on others.
These are your part
of the world's malaise.
Let each step now
be a contemplation.
Accept what has been done
and move on
with a new intention.

Solitary Lunch

Samos to Sarria

I chose a low, stone wall for my seat.
From above me an old chestnut tree
dropped a new chestnut at my feet.
Across the dirt path from where I sat,
two sparrows sang me a song.
Above, the clouds pulled back their curtain
to reveal the azure October sky.
In the pasture beyond
cows played music with their bells.
The space was green and lush.
A gnat buzzed its heart out.
The rock wall observed it all
in stony silence.
I ate and then walked on
before the place got crowded.

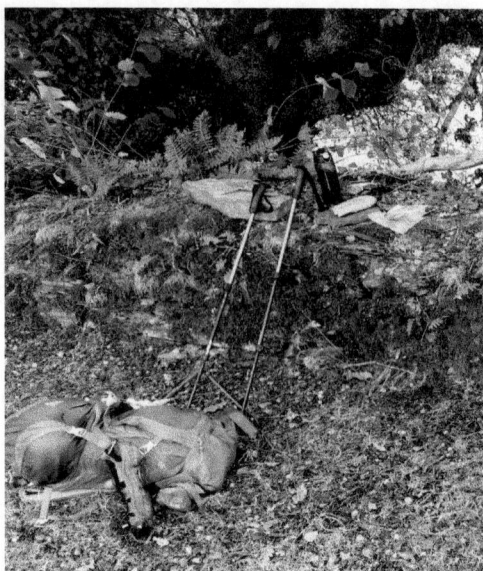

From Sarria to Santiago and Finisterre

Walls

Sarria to Barbadelo

Men build things out of stone—
buildings, bridges, roads, walls—
in hopes of a form of permanence.
Each suffers from the diminution of time.
Here on the Camino the walls
are studies of what time does
to men's fantasies of endurance.
First comes the moss, then grass.
Later heather and brambles
attach to the stony face.
Left long enough, walls
become banks, edges
with no sign of human handiwork,
absorbed into the natural landscape.
Ambition wants monuments that last.
Time's nature is impermanence.

Walking in the Rain

Barbadelo to Mercadoiro

Complain, how could you?
Look at those fields, washed by this rain.
They are a green you've never seen.
And the horizon—the mist
has turned the distant hills
into an ancient sumi-e painting.
Look how the land is lined out
in sections like an etching.
As the rain increases, we walk
under a grove of gnarled oaks
lining a stone wall, green
with moss and time and labor.
As if to test our delight
the rain shrouds our view,
drenches our clothes and
turns the path into a stream
we follow down hill.
We are soaked enough
to laugh at our expectations
of constant comfort.
Our clothes will dry.
Our skin delights in water
as the warm shower later will prove,
and the day will be remembered
long after we have forgotten
how wet we were or what town
we walked toward this day.

After Heavy Rain

Mercadorio to Portomarin

Shoes still wet
Clothes damp
Dressing slowly

Clouds still heavy
Sun hidden
But moon above

Path of puddles
Black slugs
Black slate pebbles

Long bridge over
Green flood plane
Small ancient villages

Detour to prehistoric site
Stopping for the day
Rains begin again.

Ancient Villages

Portomarin to Hospital Alta da Cruz

Pilgrims from across the known world
passed through this small village
a millennium ago
with its slate roofs and cobbled streets
echoing with cows bellowing
and dogs barking at those who pass.
Little has changed in this small place.
Dogs still bark, cows low softly,
and cats scurry into barns for milk.
Beyond here an older village lies
uncovered by archeologists.
Here the earthen walls echo
their presence too
like distant cows
and dogs baying beyond
the horizon of time.

Penance

Hospital Alta da Cruz to Melide

Three days from Santiago
and I am still wondering why
I'm walking all this way.
A thousand years off Purgatory?
I don't think so.
Forgiveness for mortal sins?
I've practiced all seven
too many times.
The penitence I seek
is for not paying attention
to this one life I have.
For example, sunrises like this one—
I've slept through or ignored thousands.
Occasionally I've noted the rings
around the moon,
but I have not learned the night's
mythology or constellations.
How many times have I watched
water bugs walk over clear streams
where the sand dances like gold flakes
and the small rocks flutter in the current?
I have just shooed away a fly
without observing its gossamer wings
and faceted eyes alert to my threats.
Those are bad enough,
but mostly I seek penance
for inattention to those
who wanted me to hear them:
children, family, dogs,
and strangers like you
who read this poem
who have stories and regrets
and seek penance too.

What I want is atonement
for not paying attention to
this abundant life of mine.

Saying the Names
Melide to Arca

As you walk on your path, here is what you must do:
with each step call out the names of those who suffer,
whose lives are slipping from them because of cancer,
disease, despair, hunger, abuse, loss, desperation,
drugs, remorse, or for the absence of love in their lives.
Some names you know because you have watched
them slowly shrink from how they were before.
Start there. Slowly, one by one say their names
to the stones waiting beneath your feet,
to the tree limbs leaning over to hear,
to the air that echoes the names you say.
Just do it, one by one say their names clearly
so that they are not forgotten in this space you walk.
There is more. There are names you have forgotten,
names you never knew, names no one knows.
Give them a name now and carefully utter it
so that forgetfulness and ignorance
are undone by your words on their behalf.
Stop, pick up a stone and give it one of their names.
Leave it on the path so that by the time you come to the end
there will be a pebbled trail of names left behind in plain view.
Pick a flower and whisper the secret name of someone
who has wanted their name spoken in love instead of hate.
Leave each flower on a post or bench for others to see.
Leave quotes, poems, or words of encouragement
all along the way you are walking.
Now say your name. Yes your name. You suffer too.
Say it aloud and listen now to all the names of those who suffer.
Let their names echo in your heart as you walk the Way.

Monte de Gozo

Arca to Monte de Gozo

We have walked all day
to this place called Mount Joy.
From here you can see
the city of Santiago spread out
and waiting for Pilgrims' arrivals.
For us the joy was in stopping
for the night to relieve our aches
and prepare for tomorrow.
The day's walk began in rain,
but the paths were not sodden
and carried us through
forests and small farms.
The Camino is not easy,
and after all these centuries
the Way has not yet become a highway.
Those who want to travel fast
take the roads to cities.
We walk and take our time.

We are Here

Monte de Gozo to Santiago

Our packs shed, here we stand
in front of the Cathedral we've walked toward
for over 500 miles with sheer delight
in spite of pain and rain
and doubts along the way.
We look for faces who've shared our path
and know that this will be our last embrace.
Inside we can almost touch the saint's
statue and in the crypt see his bones.
Here we can lay our struggles down
and leave the prayers for those
we've carried with us as we walked.
Tears now wash away our losses,
our regrets, and fears of failing
and leave us bathed in joy.
At the Mass, the great Botafumeiro
belches out incense smoke
as we watch and wonder
what it will all mean in the end.
We have our seal and scallop—
signs that have we walked the Camino.
Now as St. Francis tells us,
our pilgrimage has just begun.

What We See

Santiago

Before us we expect to see
what we imagined all along—
the Santiago Cathedral,
the one in the pictures
with tiny people
standing in the plaza
gleeful that they have finally
arrived at the final goal
of their long Camino.

Instead of solid stone
the façade is scrim,
painted to look
like the cathedral
might have looked
behind the screen.
The image hangs off
scaffolds hiding reconstruction
underway for decades.

Inside we pass the statue
of the Tree of Jesse
said to impart wisdom,
then climb behind the altar
to touch the golden statue
of Saint James whose
gold hat has been stolen,
and then descend
into the crypt where
his bones are said to lie.
Eventually we see smoke
fill the nave from the
giant censor swung
over the heads

of us pilgrims.
How to believe all this
after the image on the façade?

In the Midst of All This

Santiago to Finisterre

On the way to Finisterre
where the land ends
the hills become stony
and small fishing villages
cling to the narrow coves.
What did you expect
to find here in the rain?
The clouds roll away
and nothing is left
but the open sea.
That is your life.
There is nowhere
else to go.
In town old men
sit and smoke,
drink and play cards.
A sparrow pecks at crumbs
left on the table.
A seagull lifts off the shore
and glides away.
You are here
in the midst of all this.

The Pilgrim's Way (song)

Sung to the English tune "Foggy Foggy Dew"

The Pilgrim's way is a very long way,
It goes from the mountains to the sea.
It'll take you down and take you away
From wherever you expected to be.

CHORUS: With a pack on your back
And a staff in your hand
You'll walk for day after day.
When you find yourself
At the ocean's sand
You've come to the end of the Way.

Oh, the Camino way you'll do someday
Whenever you've lost a few pounds.
But your dinners and snacks led you astray
So it's off to the track to run rounds.

CHORUS: With a pack on your back
And a staff in your hand
You'll walk for day after day.
When you find yourself
At the ocean's sand
You've come to the end of the Way.

Oh, the Pilgrim's way is a turtle's way.
Everyone walks with a pack.
The more that you carry, the more it will weigh.
It's all got to go on your back.

CHORUS:

Oh, the Camino way is a very hard way,
It breaks your feet on the stones.
But the havoc it makes with your ego each day
Is worse than breaking your bones.

CHORUS:

Oh, the Camino way is a silent way,
Despite those Pilgrims who would talk.
When the path goes up or there're rocks on the way,
Then everyone quits talking and walks.

CHORUS:

Oh, the Pilgrim's way is a thinker's way
Yet it overturns everything you knew.
What happens on the Way is beyond what one can say,
But you know in your heart it is true.

CHORUS:

Oh, the Pilgrim's way is a friendly way.
Everyone greets you with a smile.
It's not just "Hey" but "Buen Camino" they say
As they walk with you for a while.

CHORUS:

Oh, the Camino way is a blustery way
The wind blows constantly.
If it gets in your cloak, it'll blow you away
from the Meseta all the way to the sea.

CHORUS:

Oh, the Pilgrim's way is a meandering way,
You'll pass through cities and plains.
Wherever you are, for the other you'll pray,
But neither gives relief from your pains.

CHORUS:

Oh, Santiago some say is the end of the way,
But you know in your heart it's not true.
The Pilgrim's path is just the entrée
To the rest of life's pilgrimage you'll do.

CHORUS:

Acknowledgements

Pilgrimages and writing poems are never the solitary acts we imagine them to be. Those who have gone before, those who are on the same path with us, and those who follow all enrich our experience. I wish I could acknowledge all those who have contributed to the writing of this book, but my debts go back centuries and include many whose names are lost in time.

Let me begin by thanking Glenda Bunce who invited us to walk the Camino with her. She and her friend, Anne Cushman, were our companions as we walked across Spain. For a short while Glenda's daughter, Leah Karrer, and Glenda's niece, Claire Cunningham, joined us. Along the way we met Tony and Barbara Carroll from England who became fast friends and have since walked the Camino Portugués. Tony has allowed me to use some of his photos from his Camino Francés blog.

As I walked I became friends with other pilgrims whose names I have forgotten but whose stories will be with me wherever I go. From Iceland, Sweden, Germany, Spain, Ireland, England, France or the United States, each contributed their part to the making of these poems.

One of my greatest inspirations was my friend Terry Kinnear, who walked the Camino Francés before us and showed us how to pack. He has since walked the Camino Portugués and the Camino del Norte. He has been a part of my men's group that has met weekly for 25 years. The others, John Ritchie, Curtis Wood, John Habel, Ben Bridgers, and Sandy Miller walked with me in spirit and heard me read some of these poems before I assembled the book.

The structure of the book is a travelogue from St. Jean Pied-de-Port to Finisterre. However, the inspiration grew out of the examples of early Christian pilgrims and the teachings of the Buddha. From them I learned to walk in wonder at the impermanence and delight of the world.

The design of the book, the graphics, the map, and the cover are all the work of an accomplished graphic designer at the beginning of her career. Katana Lemelin has taken my words and turned them into a book that is unlike any book of poetry I know.

My greatest appreciation goes to my family: my daughter, Courtney, her husband Mark Tomczak and their daughters, Zoë and Emma; and my son Zachary, his wife, Cheryl Roorda, and their children, Eureka and

Zephyr. They have supported me throughout this adventure and were always my cheering squad.

But without June, my companion for 54 years, I would have not had a life worth writing about. She walked the Camino with me, provided the love and affection to nurture me through the creation of this book, and contributed most of the photos as well as an artist's and proofreader's eye throughout the entire process. As always, you are the best part of my life.

About the Author

Poetry has been an essential part of Newton Smith's life for more than fifty years. Wanting to write poems was what motivated him to leave Georgia Tech and major in English at UNC Chapel Hill. After a three-year tour in the Army as a Russian linguist, he returned to UNC for his Ph.D. In graduate school he was one of the founding editors along with Russell Banks and William Matthews of *Lillabulero Magazine* and *Lillabulero Press*, then one of the significant publications of the small press movement. His dissertation was *The Origin of the Black Mountain Poets*, one of the earliest studies of that movement.

He began teaching at Western Carolina University with a focus on creative writing, contemporary poetry, modern fiction and American literature. He has taught poetry to a wide range of writers, from second grade to retirees as well as undergraduates and graduate students. His academic publications focused on the Black Mountain poets, Robert Frost, William Carlos Williams, Robert Morgan, Fred Chappell, Jim Wayne Miller, William Matthews, Russell Banks, Ron Rash and others.

He has published widely in literary magazines beginning in the 1970's, including *Southern Poetry Review, Carolina Quarterly, Ann Arbor Review* and others. His most recent poetry publications are in the *Asheville Poetry Review, Rivendale, Main Street Rag, Pisgah Review*, and *Jonah*.

Since retiring he has had time to devote to travel, gardening, Buddhist studies, mindfulness practices, and hiking in nature, especially in the Smoky Mountains. During his 2014 pilgrimage on the Camino de Santiago he wrote a poem everyday reflecting on the physical body, nature, and the spiritual as he walked along the Way.

www.ingramcontent.com/pod-product-compliance
Lightning Source LLC
LaVergne TN
LVHW021551080426
835510LV00019B/2472